halsman on the creation of photographic ideas

Philippe Halsman

halsman on the creation of photographic ideas

Ziff-Davis Publishing Company, New York

Library of Congress Catalog Card No. 60–14230

DESIGNED BY STUART AND PAULA HERMAN

PRINTED IN THE UNITED STATES OF AMERICA

For Yvonne

It is only natural to expect in a book that deals with the origin of photographic ideas an explanation of the origin of the book itself.

It started with my interest in the mental process which precedes the taking of a photograph. I found a lot of factors which could assist the birth of an unusual photographic idea. Eventually, I gave a lecture called "Obstetrics of Photographic Ideas," a title which showed my intention to help the photographer who, although pregnant with an idea, was unable to deliver it.

I received a number of requests to repeat my lecture, and many photographers assured me that my suggestions were helpful. Two of my friends, Bruce Downes and Louis Zara, suggested that I transform the lecture into a book.

I have never written a book with greater ease. All that I did was to listen to what I was saying and write it down. My publishers liked my text, but one thing all publishers have in common is an urge to change book titles. In this case, they objected to the word "Obstetrics," fearing that it would confuse the book sellers, and that my book would wind up on a medical bookshelf. I

foreword

fought like a tiger to preserve the word "Obstetrics," which, to me, had such a helpful ring. But "Creation" supplanted it. I don't mind the word creation in the mouth of a hair stylist or a dress designer because we have become accustomed to their pinnacles of grandiloquence. However, applied to the achievement of a simple mortal this word always sounds pretentious to me. And pretentiousness is one of the vices I don't enjoy.

So, before drawing any conclusion about the book, I admonish the reader to be highly original: Skip the title and read the text.

contents

How to make photographs more striking and unusual is one of the main quests of every photographer, amateur or professional.

It is a cardinal problem for the advertising photographer because each advertisement must fight for the attention of the reader. The magazine or newspaper photographer does not sell any product, yet if his pictures stop being visually interesting, they will not interest the readers—and he will soon be replaced by a more imaginative photographer.

Even amateurs who shoot for pleasure worry about the same problem. A great deal of this pleasure consists in showing their photographs. Over a billion snapshots are being made every year in this country and most of them are shown around. To emerge from this ocean of dullness, even amateur photographs have to be different.

But how? Everybody knows of course that there are some brilliant photographers who continually produce unusual photographs. Photographers who are not blessed with creativity wonder whether this gift can be acquired or taught.

Creativity and imagination are not hereditary traits, like a Hapsburg lip or a Bourbon nose. Neither are they accidents of birth, like an unusual mole or a cleft palate. They are rather what the French call *une tournure d'esprit*—a mental attitude and ability which can be directed and developed. There are very few completely sterile minds. We are all capable of producing picture ideas. Sometimes a picture idea is born in a flash of inspiration; usually it is a difficult birth, preceded by long labor pains. In search of an idea, most of

the problem

us don't know where to start nor how to go about it. This book is written for the purpose of alleviating photographers' labor pains and to help them give birth successfully to new picture ideas.

English is the most unphotogenic language I know,* but it is also the richest in intrinsic wisdom. We say: to TAKE a photograph, and we also say: to MAKE a photograph. It is curious that the language should afford this fine distinction.

When a photographer takes photographs in a strange city or photographs children at play he does not *create* a picture. He simply *takes* what is there before his eyes, ready to be snapped by his camera.

But when an art director tells a photographer that he needs a photograph of a bearded general with a monocle in his left eye, trying to drink a glass of vodka while standing on his head, the photographer cannot rush out to take this picture. Of course, there is a remote chance that he eventually might find a bearded general with a monocle in his left eye, but he will probably have to wait a long time until the general gets the sudden urge to drink vodka while standing on his head. Obviously, the only practical way of getting this picture is to hire a bearded model, assemble a general's uniform, obtain a monocle and a glass of vodka, and to direct the picture. This, in my terminology, is MAKING a picture.

taking photographs and making photographs

Almost all advertising photographs are made and not taken. Often in advertising photography the staging and directing are more important than photographic competence.

The making of photographs is, however, not the specialty of professionals only. The tourist who photographs his spouse playfully supporting the leaning tower of Pisa and the amateur who tells his children what to do in front of the camera are both involved in *making* photographs. Consciously and unconsciously, they are all searching for photographic ideas.

* My camera has never caught anyone with his tongue between his teeth, except when speaking English (probably pronouncing "th").

Those photographers who TAKE pictures belong to the candid photography school. Their greatest representative is the Frenchman Henri Cartier-Bresson who never interferes in the action he photographs and whose unobtrusiveness is so unique that it has created the legend that, at the moment of picture taking, Cartier becomes invisible. Similarly, the amateur who is photographing a baby in the crib is not making a photograph but taking it.

The problems of taking and of making photographs are completely different. In the first case, the photographer is a witness to the occurrence; in the second case, he is its creator.

The only way the candid photographer can show his imagination is in the selection of his subject and of the exact instant in which to click the shutter, in the selection of the angle, and later in cropping, printing, and layout. The main problem is the selection. Creativity is not involved. As a matter of fact, a pure candid photographer will try to exclude creativity since his principal aim is objectivity and truth.*

The analogy with literature is striking. The photographer who *takes* the picture is a visual reporter. The photographer who *makes* one is a visual author. Even if we admire creativity, we must respect the reporter with a camera—he is the true historian and sociologist of our times. His virtues are sensitivity, understanding, point of view, and speed of reflexes. But creativity and imagination have always been considered as dubious virtues in a reporter.

Therefore, this book will consider only the problem of the photographer

* We all know that written reportage always reflects the subjective feeling of the reporter; i.e., is always biased. However, the public assumes that photographic reportage reflects the objective truth. Unfortunately, even in photographic reportage objectivity is impossible. A photographer who selects, perhaps for subconscious reasons, to snap his pictures in the rare moment when Sad Sack is smiling, will have the photographic proof that Sad Sack is actually a Gay Sack.

who wants to make his photographs as freely as a writer composes his stories, not depending on what he finds before his camera but deciding himself what to put in front of it.

The idea of the picture becomes, therefore, of paramount importance. I have often been asked to evaluate the proportion of the idea content versus the photographic technique in the impact of a photograph. It is impossible to answer this question because it varies from one photograph to another. I would like, however, to mention one incident that happened to me several years ago.

In a national magazine I saw an ad which was an exact duplication of a photograph of mine previously published in *Life*. The composition, the lighting, the photographic trick I had used were copied to the smallest detail. The only difference was that instead of my famous subject the photographer had used a male model of similar appearance.

I found out which advertising agency handled the account and mailed them a registered letter, explaining that, since my original photograph was copyrighted, their ad constituted plagiarism and breach of the copyright.

I was invited to see the vice-president of the agency. He admitted forthrightly that the agency was wrong. They were aware that it was their ethical obligation to use the author of the original photograph but, because of lack of time, had used their own photographer. For the use of my idea the agency was now willing to pay an adequate fee to be fixed by me.

I explained that if the firm would have asked for my services I would have charged $1,000 for the black and white two-page-spread photograph, a rather average fee at that time. Since the photographic idea and its visual solution were copied *in toto*, the photographic execution was a job worth not more than $100. Therefore, the agency owed me $900.

The vice-president immediately agreed. A week later a representative of the firm and a notary public appeared in my studio. I had to sign a 15 release and I was given a check for $927, the additional $27 being the city sales tax. Thus we see that in this case the value of the picture idea was admitted to be nine times greater than that of its photographic execution.

But how does one go about getting an unusual photographic idea? My experience both as a father and as an obstetrician of ideas has shown me that the solution may come in either of two ways. Either it emerges gradually, after an analysis of the problem and the use of logic and deduction, or it appears spontaneously, in a flash, stimulated by something in the dark reservoir of our subconscious mind.

When the solution comes, we usually know whether it is a right or wrong solution, "a false idol or a true and noble birth," to use Socrates' words. For most people it is the birth itself which presents the greatest difficulty. To help them, I offer a system, the explanation of which begins in the next chapter.

I have assembled a set of six working rules which provide a starting point to a rational examination of the photographic problem and which, logically, should lead to a solution in the majority of instances.

In spite of psychoanalysis, we know little about the working of the subconscious mind, even less about any means of putting it to work. No system of rules can help us there. It is our subconscious which plays the most important part in every creative activity. When poets talk about inspiration, when artists of comics draw a light bulb over the hero's head to indicate the spontaneous birth of an idea, they symbolically express that the subconscious is the actual creator.

We cannot command our subconscious mind, but we can stimulate it. The second part of this book presents a system of stimulations which may make it easier for our subconscious to furnish us with ready-made solutions.

To demonstrate the working of these "systems," I wish I could illustrate this book with the most spectacular photographs of the last decade. However, even if I should be able to assemble them, how would I guess what was going on in the minds of their creators at the moments of creation? Therefore, I have resorted to the use of my own pictures. Even if they are less spectacular, at least I know the case history of each photograph.

1. the rule of the direct approach

The first rule is: try the most direct approach. Be as straightforward and plain as possible. It always makes for a strong photograph.

This rule seems self-evident, but in practice we see that many pictorial statements are made in oblique or indirect ways which only weaken their impact. Strangely, our mind often overlooks the most obvious solution. It is like searching for a secret lock in a jewel box instead of simply lifting the lid.

I remember being shown in an advertising agency a preliminary sketch for a life insurance ad. It showed a little girl happily playing with her parents. The slogan underneath asked, "Would your child have to be brought up by strangers?"

The art director and I discussed the ad. We found that the sketch illustrated the slogan in a rather oblique way. It showed the situation preceding the question: the happy child with the still-alive parents. We decided to use the direct approach and to show exactly what the slogan implied: the child being taken away by a stranger.

I hired a little professional model, four-year-old Kathy, who came with her mother. My wife would pose as the stranger and dress in black to look severe and forbidding.

part 1. rules

I shot the picture in the street. My wife took little Kathy by the hand and pulled her as if she were ready to drag her away. Kathy's mother was standing directly behind my camera, saying:

"Good-bye, Kathy, the wicked lady will take you away."

"Mummy! No! . . ." shouted Kathy toward the camera, while I snapped the picture.

The ad got one of the highest Starch ratings recorded. It had the princi- 19

pal requisites of an effective advertising picture—it was a stopper and it had simplicity, drama, and emotion. An important point: the little girl appealed for help not to somebody outside the picture but right to the camera, i.e., directly to the reader.

The next example is of more general interest. It concerns the bosom of a young French movie actress. One of the most interesting phenomena of our times is the recent spectacular career of these mammalian endowments. Today, in the choice of a leading lady, the producer usually sacrifices acting ability for nursing ability, although only few roles call for proof of the latter.

And so the march to fame of most of the international movie stars is accomplished on the strength of those parts of their anatomy which are the least fit for locomotion.

Because I was taking the picture in France, it was relatively easy to use the direct and straightforward approach. Instead of vacillating between the possibilities of asking the actress to inhale and shooting her from a low angle, or asking her to exhale and taking a plunging view, I simply and straightforwardly tore her nightgown. Thus I could again demonstrate that the direct approach usually produces a strong and dynamic picture.

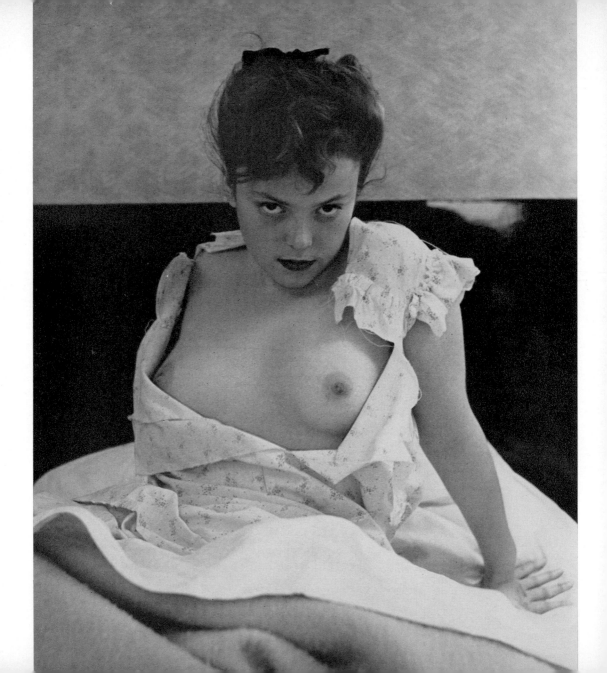

2.   the rule of the unusual technique

The second rule is very simple and evident. Often the subject of our photograph is ordinary and uninteresting. But we want to make an interesting and unusual picture! Usually, however, when we are not free to change the subject we are free to do anything we want with our photographic technique.

We can use

> an unusual lighting,
>
> an unusual angle,
>
> an unusual exposure (such as blurring the action through time exposure or freezing it by fast or multiple exposure).

We can move the camera.

We can use an unusual filter which will change the color values.

We can use an unusual lens (soft focus, extreme wide-angle, fish-eye lens, or a lens with a very long focus).

We can shoot our subject against an unusual background or with an unusual foreground.

We can distort or foreshorten our subject.

We can use an unusual composition.

We can continue our efforts after the picture has been taken: we can overdevelop or underdevelop, reticulate the emulsion or solarize it.

We can continue to use our imagination while we enlarge the photograph:

> We can crop our image in an unusual way.
>
> We can make a very dark dramatic print or make it look light and soft like a pencil drawing.
>
> We can use paper of very high or very low contrast.
>
> We can diffuse or distort the picture.

23

We can use a texture screen or we can overprint another negative.
We can use a small mirror at the enlarger lens and make a print
which mirrors itself,
etc., etc.

Even when the photograph is finished, we can insist on an unusual layout.

I have seen rather ordinary looking color photographs made interesting by printing; by using only two or three of the four color plates.

The technical possibilities of making a picture look unusual are so great that they cannot be exhausted in one chapter; there have been entire books written on photographic technique and trick photography.

The points which I specified are, however, not only tricks. They are mentioned for the purpose of reminding you of a technical improvement that might be otherwise overlooked and to show you how wide your choice of possibilities is.

When I speak, for example, of using an unusual lighting, you should not assume that I simply suggest lowering the main light as much as possible. No. I want you to think of all the possibilities this term implies: shooting the subject at dusk, or at night, against a sunset, using colored lights with color film, throwing a pattern of shadows, shooting the subject as a silhouette, and many more.

When I mention, for instance, shooting against an unusual background, I don't mean only the unusual background that we can produce in our home or our studio. Bert Stern went to Egypt to photograph a vodka glass in front of the Great Pyramid.

As an example of making the picture more arresting through use of an unusual angle, a photograph of one of my favorite subjects, the Spanish surrealist Salvador Dali, is printed on the opposite page. I had photographed his face from so many points of view that it was difficult for me to think of

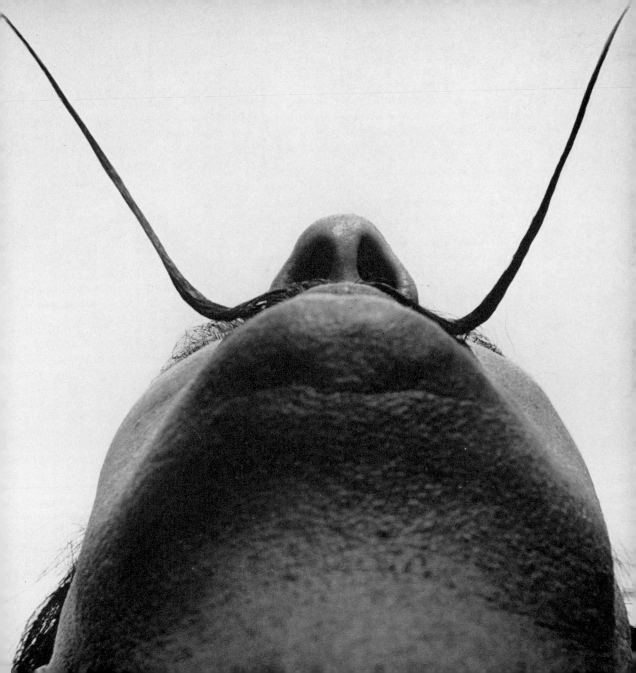

a completely new aspect. However, an exceedingly low angle did the job.

Once, for an advertising agency, I had to photograph the test run of an automobile through water. It has become tradition in Detroit to test a new car by driving it through a water trough without stalling the engine. I had seen hundreds of such photographs. On both sides of the car the splashing water looks like two enormous wings. These photographs all look alike; the only thing that varies is the make of the car.

To make this traditional picture more unusual, I decided to use unusual lighting, and to shoot at dusk. My camera had flash synchronization, and I placed one flashbulb on each side of the trough so that the light would shine through the water wings and illuminate them.

I shot the picture six times, showing heroism beyond the call of duty (which, by the way, remained—as usual—completely unappreciated). It was November and very cold. Every time, a split second after shooting the picture, a wall of water would hit and completely drench me and my camera. My only satisfaction was that I did not get a cold, which confirmed my notion that one catches colds not from bad weather but from good friends.

3. the rule of the added unusual feature

The third rule is a logical extension of the second. Instead of concentrating on photographic technique (or after we have exhausted its possibilities), we can try to introduce an interesting feature or prop into our photographs.

Advertising photography gives us a few strikingly successful examples of this method: the eye-patch of the Hathaway shirt, the bearded Schweppes Commander, and the Marlboro tattoo. None of these elements has anything to do with the subject of the photograph. Each has been deliberately introduced for one purpose only: to catch our attention. The eye-patch does not

lengthen the wearability of a shirt, Commander Whitehead's beard adds nothing to the effervescence of the quinine water, and a tattoo on the hand does not improve the taste of a cigarette.

The effectiveness of these features is magnified by the fact that they are not only simple attention-getters, they are also symbols which wield a strange influence on our subconscious mind.

The Marlboro tattoo stands for virility and adventure. The eye-patch is a highly disturbing Freudian symbol which, like King Oedipus piercing his own eyes, is related, as any psychoanalyst will point out, to the castration complex. And, naturally, Commander Whitehead's bushy beard has definite Freudian overtones, or should I say undertones?

The added attention-getting feature does not always have to be an object. It may also be an attention-getting action.

A few years ago, I had to photograph a group of five famous choreographers for *Life* magazine. It is difficult to make an interesting photograph of a group of five people. I asked one of the choreographers to jump, and his figure suspended in mid-air makes this group less commonplace.

4.   the rule of the missing feature

While the previous rule suggested an addition of an unusual feature, the fourth rule suggests just the contrary: the omission of a feature in a photograph. The fact that something which should be there is missing makes a picture disturbing and attention-getting.

This phenomenon explains the success of one of my Churchill pictures. The missing feature is, of course, the face. The onlooker is disturbed, his curiosity is aroused; then, with relief, he solves the visual puzzle. It is unmistakably Sir Winston! I could have shown his face, but then the photo- **29**

graph would have been commonplace. By showing less of Sir Winston, I have gotten more of the essence of Churchill.

The photograph of Dali in my book *Dali's Mustache* is based on the same principle. Although, except for the mustache, the face is blank, we immediately recognize the famous Spaniard. My question: "Why do you wear a mustache, Salvador?" is answered with this photograph and Dali's words: "In order to pass unobserved," meaning, naturally, that the public is so flabbergasted by this hairy protuberance that it does not notice the real Dali behind it. By the way, this picture has become for me the symbol of Dali's tragedy. His critics don't see the man and his work behind the whimsey and eccentricity of his behavior.

The third example of this rule is a tale with a rather ironic twist, but not unfamiliar to most photographers. In one respect my experience reminded me of the *Life* photographer who for many weeks worked to produce an essay on the Mississippi River. He photographed the river from boats, from airplanes, and from the rattlesnake-infested swamps on its borders. Once their team killed and cooked a rattlesnake, an event which the photographer recorded with his camera. When he finally returned to the magazine with hundreds of photographs of the river, out went the essay on the Mississippi and in went the article "How to Kill and Cook a Rattlesnake."

My story was similar. I was on assignment for *Life* to shoot an international meet of underwater ballet swimmers. For three days I photographed the girls doing the most complicated wheels and tricks under water. Once, during a break, the winning Canadian team came to the surface to gulp for air. From the bottom of the pool I photographed them treading water. This artless feat was given the place of honor in print. The impact of the missing feature—a dozen girls without heads—was too powerful. Or was it because the editors had finally found their image of the ideal woman, all body and no head?

5.   the rule of compounded features

Sometimes you find an idea which adds originality to your photograph, but you realize that this idea is too weak to make it sufficiently unusual. The fifth rule suggests not simply to disregard this idea but to try to find an additional one. By combining two or more ideas, which by themselves are insufficient, by developing and compounding them, it is often possible to achieve an end result which is satisfying.

No nightclub would hire a violinist whose playing was only passable or an acrobat whose only ability was standing on his head. But a passable violinist, playing while standing on his head, could immediately find a booking. The combination of two mediocre features would have become an unusual act.

The photograph on the following page is an example of the application of this rule. It is also taken from *Dali's Mustache*, which I quote so often because the entire book was nothing but an exercise in imagination. I had only one subject, Dali's mustache, and had to produce thirty-two interesting and unusual pictures. The book is now out of print and a collector's item. I must, however, confess, that it was not entirely a publishing success. The publishers and I had overestimated the interest of the American public in Dali's mustache.

In my efforts to make unusual photographs of the mustache, I wanted to show it on fire or under water. The photograph of Dali's burning mustache was not sufficiently spectacular to deserve publication, since the book had only black-and-white illustrations and one could not see the color of the flames.

To photograph the mustache under water, I asked Dali to put his head in a glass tank filled with water. His mustache drooped and looked rather funny. But it was not enough to fill me with enthusiasm. I gave Dali some

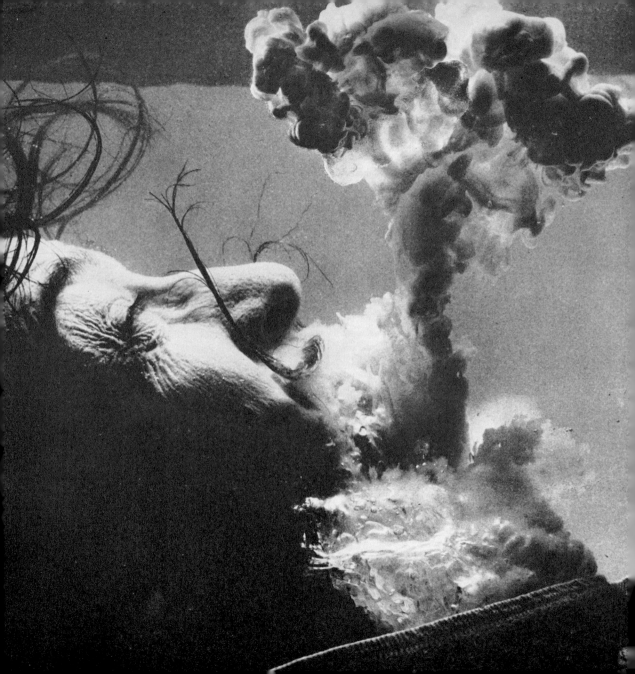

milk, which he squirted out of his mouth when he again put his head under water. It produced a kind of atomic mushroom cloud. Through the combination of two features, I had a sufficiently unusual photograph.

6.　the rule of the literal or ideographic method

Often the photographer finds himself in a position where he has to illustrate a caption or wants to express an idea visually. For a given statement he has to invent an image.

Rule No. 6 advises trying literally to translate the very words of the statement into images—therefore, the "literal" method. Sometimes it is not the words but the idea of the statement which is expressed in a visual image. This image becomes a kind of ideograph—consequently, "ideographic" method. The result is usually a very effective solution which combines a visual image with an image created by words and is therefore not easily forgotten by the onlooker.

The Chinese or Japanese alphabet* is entirely based on this principle. It originally started with hieroglyphics, i.e., every word was represented by a picture. Then the picture was condensed to a sign. Now, to write the words "ear" or "eye" one draws the sign symbolizing the ear or the eye. More complicated words are written by combining two or more signs into one sign. This combination of signs is called an "ideograph."

For instance, the ideograph for "listening" is a combination of the sign "ear" and the sign "door." The ideograph for "weeping" is the combined signs "eye" and "water."

* The Chinese alphabet was introduced in Japan about 400 A.D.

Other examples:

The sign for "dog" and the sign for "mouth" combined give "barking."

The sign for "bird" and the sign for "mouth" combined give "singing."

The sign for "knife" and the sign for "heart" combined give "sorrow," and so on.

In contrast to our alphabet, which is acoustic (our letters are transcriptions of sound), the Chinese alphabet is visual. It is a kind of shorthand of images, and thus the thinking of the intelligentsia of the Orient is visually conditioned. This explains why we often don't completely understand Oriental poetry. Half of its beauty is visual and lies in the combination and interplay of the ideographs. This visual conditioning of thinking explains also the so-called "innate" gift of the Orientals for composition, flower arrangements, decoration, etc.

Another extraordinary advantage of this alphabet is that people of different tongues can use it. The Chinese of the North and the Chinese of the South know which object the ideograph represents, although sometimes the spoken word for it is different in the two dialects. This alphabet could be an international script, understood by all the people of the globe. But do we need it? We have already an international visual medium of communication which does not know any language barriers: photography.

Let me illustrate the use of the ideographic method with a few examples.

Some time ago, *Life* commissioned me to take a color photograph of Zsa Zsa Gabor with her ghost writer Gerold Frank for possible use as a *Life* cover. As usual, the execution was left entirely to the photographer.

Frank's method of ghostwriting was to ask probing questions and record Zsa Zsa's answers on tape which later became the basis for his book of her memoirs.

As I had immediately rejected the idea of a formal double portrait as hackneyed, I decided to show Frank's method of working. I shot Frank's

LIFE

BIGGEST ANIMAL RESCUE OPERATION SINCE NOAH

POPULAR WORLD OF ANTIQUES

NOW 19¢

ZSA ZSA GABOR AND HER FAMOUS GHOST

JUNE 29, 1959 **19** CENTS

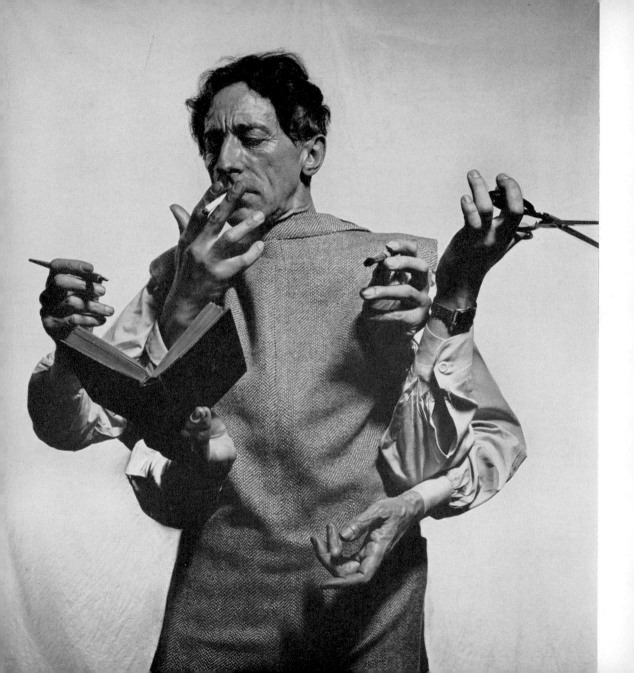

face leaning over the tape recorder in the foreground and Zsa Zsa's figure in the background. Then I reversed the situation and had Zsa Zsa lying on a couch in the foreground and Frank with the tape recorder, sitting like a psychoanalyst in the background.

But before taking these two pictures I had used the literal or ideographic approach to visually translate the idea "ghost writer." In my photograph I kept the actress in the foreground and placed the writer behind a semi-transparent tulle curtain which made him look like a ghost.

This was, of course, the version that was selected for the cover (which, by the way, was my 86th *Life* cover). The words: "Zsa Zsa Gabor and her Ghost writer Gerold Frank" were imprinted on it—almost superfluously, since they only repeated what was already literally spelled out by the picture.

Once, while photographing the French poet Jean Cocteau, I wanted to emphasize his versatility. He not only wrote the script for his movie, but he also directed it, designed the sets and the costumes, painted the scenery, and so on. The problem was to show him in a photograph as Jack-of-all-trades. The Russian expression for this phrase came to my mind, "*Master na vse ruki*," which means, literally, "master of all hands." I hid two other people behind Cocteau and showed him with six hands, each hand doing something different.

Two years ago, I was asked by Farrar, Straus & Cudahy to make a book jacket for Alberto Moravia's book *Two Women*. The jacket won an award for the best book cover of the year, and the girl on the jacket was offered several movie contracts.

A year later, I met one of the publishers, Roger Straus, who told me how much Moravia had liked the jacket. "We are publishing a new book of his, *The Wayward Wife*, and again we would like you to do the jacket. Have you an idea for it?" he asked.

Immediately, a sort of an ideograph for this title flashed in my mind and I said, "I see a lonely road and a nude girl on it." "That is a marvelous idea," replied the publisher, "but where will you get the nude girl?"

I answered, "Roger, my only worry is, where will I get the lonely road!"

This jacket, too, had an interesting story. *The New York Times* did not consider at all the nude as fit to print. The body of the girl was covered not with a fig leaf but with a circular sign showing the price of the book. The *Herald Tribune* was more progressive and did not bowdlerize my photograph.

Many book reviews commented on the jacket. The review in the *New Yorker* was one page long, half of it about the jacket. In *Time* magazine only a third of the generally favorable review was devoted to the jacket photograph, but the critic preferred it to the text.

In the first part of the book I discussed rules which apply to the rational and logical part of our thinking. But sometimes our creativeness seems to be completely spontaneous. The ideas, the solutions, appear suddenly from our subconscious as if they had been there waiting to be born. We cannot produce them at will by logical means. However, there are other means of stimulating their birth, and the second portion of this book is about the stimulations which provoke it.

1. stimulation by brainstorming

Madison Avenue contends that the creation of striking and unusual ideas is its daily business. It is not surprising, therefore, that a highly advertised method of generating ideas was invented by one of the largest advertising companies, BBD&O. The inventor of this method, Alex Osborn (the O in BBD&O), calls it brainstorming. He describes the technique of brainstorming in his book *Applied Imagination.*

This method has been accepted by many other agencies and has spread to industry and even to the armed forces. Brainstorming sessions are regularly conducted in the BBD&O agency. Ten to fifteen people meet in a rather small room around a big table. In the hierarchy of the agency these people have approximately the same rank, consequently they don't intimidate each other. The participants are encouraged to voice even the most foolish-sounding suggestions, because

part 2. stimulations

each suggestion is supposed to stimulate and generate the birth of other suggestions. Alex Osborn boasts that a brainstorming session often produces over a hundred different solutions.

The illustration on page 47 shows an actual BBD&O brainstorming **45** session. One recognizes on the right William Pleuthner, BBD&O vice-president in charge of brainstorming, conducting the session.

Opinion about the efficiency of brainstorming is divided. My own opinion takes the middle road. On one hand, I am aware of the fact that, although brainstorming sessions often do produce a hundred solutions, frequently none of them is usable. On the other hand, I remember what a psychologist once told me about the famous Rodin statue, "The Thinker." "Look at him," he said, "how hard he strains for a thought! But I am sure that in his head there is nothing but a vacuum. This is not the way to get an idea."

Although I have never participated in brainstorming sessions with ten or more participants, I find that as a rule I am more productive when I discuss the problem with someone than when I am alone. One reason is psychological. You are not alone, but you face someone who serves you as a sounding board, prods you, and expects an answer. The second reason is physiological. Your system is stimulated by the challenge of the discussion. There is more adrenalin in your blood, more blood flows through the brain, and, like an engine that gets more gas, your brain becomes more productive. Consequently, discussions with an editor, with an art director, with a friend, and even with my own wife are, for me, sufficient substitutes for brainstorming. Their prodding, their suggestions and objections, their answers, and their waiting for my reply are the stimulations I need.

Sometimes prodding alone is enough. Once after a show I found myself in a restaurant face to face with a horse-faced gentleman. I recognized him as my favorite French comedian, and because I had seen him so often on the screen I had the feeling that I knew him personally.

"Fernandel! How long have you been here?" I exclaimed.

Fernandel very courteously answered, "I just arrived to see the Marcel Cerdan—La Motta fight and I am leaving tomorrow for Canada. But in a

week I will be back in New York for two days."

Suddenly, I realized that I was only a stranger to him. I apologized blushingly and left. My wife, who was with me, said on the way home, "Philippe, you must photograph him for a magazine."

"It's useless," I said. "He is completely unknown here."

"So make him known!" prodded my wife. "Make him interesting."

"What is so interesting about him?" I said, and thought: "Perhaps I'll ask him to act out the fight between Cerdan and La Motta?—But when the story appears, the fight will already be a dead fish."

But my loyal wife continued with her usual feminine logic, "So make up something interesting."

I was starting to get cross with her, when an idea flashed in my mind. "I know what I'll do," I said. "I will interview Fernandel about America, and he will answer with his facial expressions only!"

Now that we have seen dozens of similar picture stories, my idea does not seem too original. But although photographs of people followed by captions explaining what the people were saying are almost as old as photography itself, nobody before had used the device of printing a question on one page and letting the reader, on turning the page, find the answer in a silent photograph. Since ideas are not patentable, an avalanche of imitations of *The Frenchman* flooded the market: *The Baby, The Comedian, The Secretary, The Swede, The Candidate, The Gams,* etc.

But let me return to my story, which has all the characteristics of a brainstorming session with the only difference that there were never more than two brainstorm-troopers in action.

In the following days, I started to write down questions: How do you like America? What do you think about the international situation? (I knew that a sour expression would be valid for many years to come.) What do you think about the American sweater girls? Do you realize that last year two and one-half million falsies were sold here? (As you see, it was just the beginning of this expanding industry.) Have you tasted our California champagne? etc.

Fernandel arrived in New York and came to my studio. Using my strobe lights and a Rollei, I made eighty-four shots of his answers to a dozen of my questions. I was curious whether the great comedian himself would suggest an interesting question. Fernandel was willing. "Ask me whether I have seen the skyscrapers."

Eagerly I asked, "Have you seen the skyscrapers?"

Fernandel looked up as if he were observing the skyscrapers. It was a logical thing to do, only it was not funny. I shot it anyway.

The entire sitting had taken fifty-five minutes. Twelve of the pictures with my questions were published in *Life* magazine. My friend, the publisher Richard Simon, saw the pictures and said, "I would like to make a book out of them."

"But there are not enough photographs," I objected.

"Do you have any rejects?"

"Yes, I made over eighty shots."

Dick looked at them and decided, "There is enough for a book."

Again I objected, "But how about the questions? All the possibilities are already exhausted."

Dick smiled. "Don't worry. I will take care of it."

At Simon & Schuster's, my photographs were turned over to a professional writer whose specialty was suggesting captions for cartoons. The writer produced eighty questions which fit the photographs perfectly, but made no one laugh.

Dick Simon called for me. He took out the photograph of Fernandel, looking at the invisible skyscrapers and asked, "Do you have any ideas for a funny question?"

Inexperienced in brainstorming as I was and certain that I had milked dry all the possibilities, I said, "There aren't any."

"Well," said Dick, "one could ask Fernandel how much is two and two."

I was stunned. It *was* a funny question. Suddenly, where I had only seen Fernandel looking up, I saw him contemplating a problem with indecision.

"Dick," I said, "my pictures are the interview of a slightly frivolous Frenchman by a slightly puritanical American. I could not possibly ask him a problem in arithmetic. Suppose, however, I ask him, 'If you saw your mother-in-law drowning, would you try to save her?' "

Dick looked at the indecision in Fernandel's face and laughed.

"No," I said, "let's keep the mothers-in-law out. I must ask him something that would confound a Frenchman, especially a Frenchman from Marseilles. I know!" I exclaimed, "What would you rather give up, women or garlic?"

Dick Simon took the batch of photographs, put it under my arm, and said, "You write the rest of the questions."

This happening taught me the lesson that an unusable, even sometimes foolish, suggestion can be the stimulus for a useful solution; that each solution can be more and more improved; and, finally, that one should never think that one has milked a problem dry of solutions. Relax for a while and then try again. As any milkmaid will tell you: a new squeeze will produce a new squirt.

This anecdote shows my response to prodding. I would like now to tell the story of an instance where I was the prodder. Several years ago, a Spanish editor approached Salvador Dali with the proposition of publishing a book of my photographs of Dali. We looked over the collection of these pictures and, with customary shrewdness, Dali remarked that an unusual photograph of a female nude would add to the attractiveness of the book.

But what kind of a photograph?

"Let us impress the public by the sheer number of nudes. Suppose we had a half dozen of them," I suggested.

"A splendid idea," said Dali, "but what will they be doing?"

That was a ticklish problem, and there was a silence.

"How about the temptation of St. Anthony?" I asked. St. Anthony suffered, like many of us who are not saints, from erotic hallucinations.

"Old fashioned and corny," answered Dali. "The Renaissance painters have done it to death."

We left without having found a solution.

The next morning, my telephone rang. "Yesterday you made an excellent suggestion about St. Anthony!" said Dali's voice.

I was surprised. "But you did not like it!"

"Yes, but later I came to the conclusion that deep in his idea of mortal sin was hidden the idea of death. I have just finished a drawing of seven nudes. If you look at it from afar, you see a death's head, a symbol of what St. Anthony saw in carnal sin."

I booked seven nude models, but to be on the safe side I also hired two spare nudes. The sitting took three and a half hours. I had as guests a couple of editors. One of them was so impressed that he later quit his profession and became a photographer.

Although the photograph carried a highly moral message and was so cleverly composed that all the strategic points our Post Office so valiantly struggles with were covered, no national magazine dared to print it. Eventually, it was published in a photography annual.

I will finish this lengthy section on stimulation with the story of a discussion which was a brainstorming session *en miniature*.

One day Dali returned from Spain with a new painting. It showed Mrs. Dali as Leda being embraced by a swan. But the swan embraced her without actually touching her. Mrs. Dali was not really sitting on a pedestal but

rather floating above it, and even the wave breaking against the shore, through a miraculous tour de force, was not in contact with the bottom of the sea.

"Dali," I asked, "why do you call this painting 'Leda Atomica'?"

"I became aware that an atom is not an indivisible piece of matter," he said, "but consists of a nucleus, and of protons, neutrons, electrons, and other junk, all rotating in suspension around the nucleus. Since everything consists of atoms, everything is in suspension. Being the most modern painter of our times, I have to paint everything as it is—in suspension."

The next morning I phoned Dali. "I have an idea for a photograph called 'Dali Atomicus.' It shows you in mid-air, painting. Everything in the photograph is in suspension; for instance, the easel with the canvas. But I cannot impose on you the subject of your painting. All I can say—it too must be in suspension."

"That is a sublime idea. Please come to my hotel and let us discuss it."

In the bar of the Hotel St. Regis, we sat down behind a Champagne cocktail and a glass of Vichy water.

"I have a marvellous idea," said Dali, "we take a duck, *on lui f . . . de la dynamite dans le derrière* (one stuffs some dynamite into its behind), the duck explodes, I jump, and you take the picture. Everything is in suspension."

"Dali," I exclaimed, "we will be arrested immediately."

Dali hit himself on the head. "I always forget that I am in America! We have to find something else."

I waited. Then Dali said: "Have you seen Edgerton's photograph of a milk drop? When it hits the milk, it looks like a little crown."*

"Yes," I said, surprised that he remembered this photograph.

"We will take a bucket of milk and throw a cat in it."

54   * An example of #2. Stimulation by memory.

"Let us take water, because milk is not transparent," I objected. "We won't see the immersed half of the cat. His protruding half will also be covered by splashing milk, and we won't be able to see what it is."

"Don't you understand that milk has just the right viscosity?"

We continued the argument, and I saw that I could not win it by appealing to his reason. So I made an appeal to his heart.

"Dali, little children are starving in Europe because they cannot get milk. (It was shortly after the end of World War II.) The photograph will be published there, and the Europeans will see that we use milk to drench cats."

Dali's heart was vulnerable. "You are right," he said tragically. "We will have to use water." After a thoughtful silence he added, "But we will not throw the cat in the water. We will hurl it in the air and throw the water at it."

On the day of the shooting I had three cats ready. We started with one, but ambition soon prompted us to use all of them at once. I counted; at "three," three helpers hurled the cats and a fourth helper threw the water. While the cats and water traveled in the air, I counted "four," Dali jumped, and I took the picture. Then I went to the darkroom and developed the film. My helpers wiped clean the studio floor and gathered the cats. I soon appeared with the wet film and explained why we had to shoot another time. Six hours and twenty-eight throws later, the result satisfied my striving for perfection. My assistants and I were wet, dirty, and near complete exhaustion—only the cats still looked like new.

The photograph appeared on a double page in *Life* and was immediately pirated everywhere. It appeared without payment in Europe, Japan, South America, South Africa, and Australia. I was told by friends that it was shown in newsreels in Italy and Spain, the movie camera scanning its details and the narrator giving his commentary. The picture is included in Steichen's selection, *Photography in Retrospect*.

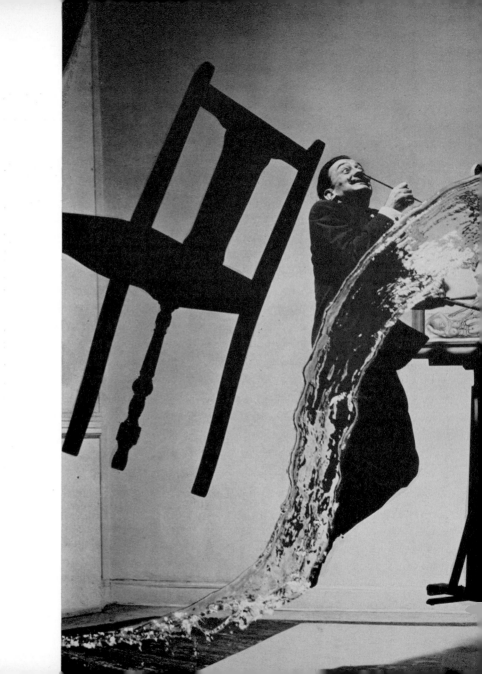

2.   stimulation by memory

The roots of most of our ideas draw from the great reservoir of our memory. Each book we read, each play or movie we see, each symphony we hear, each photograph or painting we study enriches our possibilities as an artist and as a human being. But when we put our memory to use, often we cannot avoid imitation.

How objectionable is imitation? The word "imitator" has a bad sound. But we must recognize that there are two kinds of imitation.

When imitation means solely copying somebody else's work, it is wrong and worthless. But when imitation means stimulation which develops something that exists and adds to its elements something that is new and personal, it is the kind of imitation that is responsible for the entire progress of our technology and civilization.

If we fly jet planes now, it is only because two generations of designers imitated existing designs and added something of their own. The entire Renaissance was nothing but an imitation of the suddenly rediscovered classical art of Rome and Greece. The great painter Pablo Picasso started by imitating first his teachers, then his Parisian colleagues. Later his entire work underwent a change because of the influence of African art, Minoan art, and a dozen other primitive arts. Recently, he has created a number of astonishing canvases which have as their theme a frank imitation of another great Spanish master, Velasquez. As their subject matter, he used Velasquez' "Las Meniñas" ("The Maids of Honor") as seen by his own abstract and distorting eye. The remarkable thing, however, is that this painter who in his life has imitated so much and so many is doubtless the most creative and the most original artist of our time.

We all agree that slavish copying is sterile and worthless. But we must also have the courage to admit that, as long as one adds his own values, conscious or subconscious imitation is part of the creative process. "Genius borrows nobly," says Emerson.

If in a photograph of a mother with child the radiance of mother love reminds you of one of Raphael's masterworks, it might be a good photograph. But if the photographer took two models, made them up to resemble the original subjects, drew a similar background, and directed the models to assume the identical pose, the result would always be trash and a travesty of the original work.

Once I was on a tiny uninhabited island with three little girls and their parents. It was terribly hot, and since we were alone, the children took off their bathing suits. Except for their little bottoms, they were as brown as a berry, and I wanted very much to photograph the three of them. But how? Lying down, or running, or playing? In the backlog of my memory flashed "The Three Graces" by Raphael. I put the taller girl in the middle and asked her to protect the two little ones. With the title "The Tail End of Summer" **59**

the picture was published on the cover of the British magazine *Stop*.

It is interesting to note that in his painting "The Three Graces" Raphael imitated a then recently discovered Roman fresco, which in its turn was nothing but a representation of a famous, since lost, Greek sculpture.

Once I wanted to make a portrait of Jean Cocteau which would convey that the French poet was the creator of the movie *The Eagle Has Two Heads*. Incontestably, I must have had the two-faced Roman god Janus in my mind when I edge-lit Cocteau's profile, in order to later sandwich two negatives. I must confess that I did not expect a third monstrous face to appear in the middle of the two profiles. When, however, in the darkroom I noticed this accidental gift, I moved the two negatives until I got the maximum effect. It is interesting to note that, since the publication of this photograph, Cocteau often draws in lieu of a signature two crisscrossing profiles with a third face appearing in the middle. I have often heard people comment how original this signature is.

At times, recollections which stimulate us are completely subconscious. A number of years after the Cocteau photograph had appeared in *Life*, one of the *Life* art directors called me. He needed an illustration for an article which explained that men and women in our American civilization become more and more similar: the men become more feminine and the women more masculine—until the two sexes almost merge.

He drew me a sketch of two merging profiles, overlapping each other, and I exclaimed, "I see, it is the idea of my Cocteau portrait."

Only when I drew a sketch of my photograph did the art director remember it. "But it is a completely different idea," he said. "In my case the two heads penetrate each other."

I did not argue. Instead of edge-lighting only the profiles of my two models, I also directed my spotlights on the backs of their heads. Then I sandwiched the negatives, as I did with Cocteau, and printed my picture. **61**

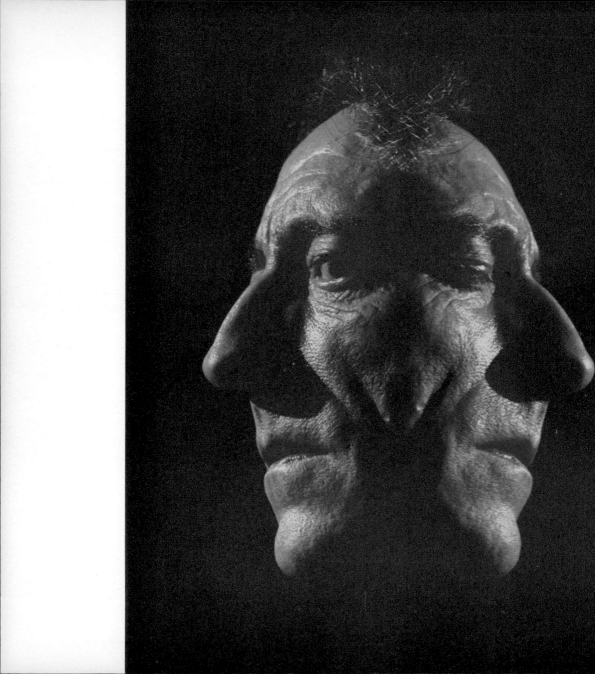

3.　stimulation by knowledge

In the previous chapter we have seen how memory can trigger our imagination. But our mind also contains a different kind of information: knowledge of things whose outcome and effect we can predict. Instead of looking backwards, this knowledge looks to the future for effects which we can use in our photograph.

When the famous photographer Gjon Mili (who, by the way, started his career as an electrical engineer) photographed Picasso, he put in the painter's hand an electric flashlight and, in the darkened room, asked him to draw a bull in the air.

Mili knew beforehand that by opening the camera shutter he could capture on film the fleeting image created by Picasso's flashlight. In the middle of this action Mili fired his speedlights, and the film also registered the room and Picasso in the act of drawing the bull.

Tiny flashlights attached to moving wrists and ankles of sportsmen or to moving machinery had been used before to delineate motion, but never to register a drawing. When Mili gave Picasso the flashlight he was not stimulated by an image in his memory but by the knowledge of what would happen.

Stimulated by this newly invented art-form, Drawing with Light, Dali and I experimented in another nonexistent art form: Sculpture with Light. Wearing a black mask and completely covered with black, in front of a black background, Dali held and moved a glowing sphere and a glowing cylinder, producing strange-looking sculptures on the film in my camera.

Once, on a Detroit proving ground, I was taking pictures of the latest models of the Chrysler line. The five cars—a Plymouth, a Dodge, a DeSoto, a Chrysler and an Imperial—were lined up for me on the test track. It was a dull-looking picture, and I felt a desire to shoot the cars rushing toward

the camera. It would have been safe if I could have hidden the camera in a deep enough hole and released it electrically from the sideline. But I had only fifteen minutes to make this shot—not enough time to dig a hole in a cement test track.

I filled my negative with the five cars, stopped down the lens completely, set the shutter on time and shouted, "One, two, three!"

At "three!" the five cars went as fast as they could—*backwards*. I exposed for two seconds. Although I had never tried it previously, I knew beforehand that the film would not know in which direction the cars were moving. When the senior art director of the agency saw the photograph his first question was, "And what happened to the photographer?"

4.   stimulation by an object

A photographer sees more than other people do. He is always on the lookout for something interesting. Interesting objects cannot only make our photographs more interesting, but they are sometimes capable of stimulating us to make an unusual photograph. The recipe is: if you have such an object give some thought to it.

Once after a portrait sitting, a glamorous Hollywood star left her paraphernalia in my studio: a couple of false eyelashes, a wig, and, naturally, a pair of falsies. This gave me an idea. I phoned my dentist and asked him to lend me some false teeth. I combined everything into an image which I called "The Essence of Glamour," and photographed it. When I showed the result to my brother-in-law, who like every Frenchman is a great connoisseur of women, he remarked, "You know, she has a certain charm."

68 The only one who was outraged about this photograph was Dr. Ordman,

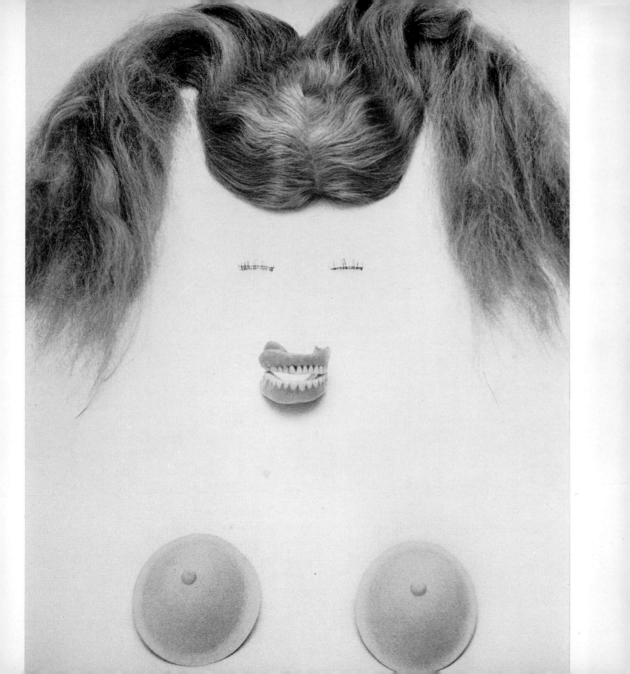

my dentist. "Do you know what you have done?" he asked. "She has her lowers in place of her uppers."

Another time I had a knight's armor left after a sitting for an advertising photograph. The old notion of the knight in shining armor protecting the virtue of a fair maiden gave me the idea for the photograph on page 71 in which the roles are slightly reversed. The fair maiden seems to be impatiently looking for a can opener.

It is not necessary to have these objects in your studio or in your home. A few years ago I photographed the Security Council hall in the UN. The enormous conference table impressed me and started me thinking. The destinies of many countries will be figuratively lying on this table, and one day the discussions might involve the question of our life and death. I saw my body lying on the table and the delegates arguing over it.

I looked around. There was nobody in the conference room. My camera was set. I lay down on the table and asked my assistant to release the shutter.

I hope one day this photograph will be published with the caption: "Beware! The corpse on the conference table might be your own!"

5. stimulation by the photograph itself

It is interesting that a frequent source of stimulation is the finished photograph. How often does it happen that a photographer looking at the end result of his efforts exclaims, "Now I know what I should have done!" Unfortunately, this stimulation often comes when it is too late to do anything about it.

The obvious advice is: look for stimulation *before* it is too late. Try to sketch the photograph beforehand or, at least, visualize it in all its details.

Often it is of great help to make a Polaroid picture during the sitting. The study of this Polaroid shot might trigger a new idea.

Not always, however, does the stimulation coming from a finished photograph resemble crying over spilled milk. Sometimes such stimulation causes one to see the possibility of transforming the picture into something new and different.

I will show later two examples of this transformation, but first I want to tell how the stimulation coming from a set of my own pictures involved me in a project which after six years of shooting led me to the publication of *Philippe Halsman's Jump Book*. Using jump photographs of 176 famous people, I established a new science which I called "Jumpology." Jumpology permits us to interpret the character of the jumper through the analysis of his jump.

When people ask me, "What gave you the idea for this new theory?" I usually answer with touching humility, "Probably my genius."

In reality, however, it was stimulation No. 5. I was engaged at that time in making a series of photographs of a number of NBC comedians. In one sitting I would make about a hundred different photographs usable for all kinds of publicity and advertising. I asked the comedians to dance, to tell stories, to make faces, and also to jump. Once, as a possibility for a picture layout, I assembled jump photographs of a dozen comedians. Suddenly, I saw in these finished photographs that each comedian had jumped in character. There was Jimmy Durante, flapping his arms like a big-nosed bird; there was Jack Carson, a little too heavy, but jumping out of his clothes and showing that inside he felt young and slender. Dave Garroway, holding his arms in a harmonious circle, seemed to say "Peace" to everybody; and Milton Berle, in reality bright and clever, knocked himself out trying to look like a fool.

"All right," I said to myself, "comedians are used to expressing themselves, but how is it with other people? Will their characters too become apparent?" I started to ask every known personality I photographed to jump. Every new jump confirmed my conclusion that in a jump the mask falls and the real self becomes visible.

This story shows how a dozen photographs stimulated me to produce a new theory and publish a book.

The following example shows how a photograph stimulated me to create its improved version.

Recently, in Hollywood, I photographed a new and beautiful French movie actress. All her previous photographs showed her in elegant clothes. Therefore, and because her stage name sounded like the name of an old monks' order, I asked her to bring a monk's habit for the sitting. I found her intriguing; something seemed to be hidden behind her façade of reserve and polite distinction.

To better understand her, I asked her to jump and got an interesting picture. First, it showed that behind the façade of sophisticated worldliness was hidden a little scared girl; second, her silhouette in monk's clothes made her look like a strange witch floating in the sky. The fact, however, that witches usually schedule their flights for nighttime gave me an idea. I printed the negative again, holding back her face and giving the photograph an eerie nightlike feeling—an effect that I had not at all originally planned.

When I photographed Dali for the book *Dali's Mustache*, I asked him whether his mustache could not take the form of an interrogation mark.

"Everything is possible with Hungarian mustache wax," answered Dali, and built two interrogation marks out of his mustache. In the photograph, the interrogation marks seemed to form an "S." Looking at the print, Dali suddenly had an inspiration. He put two thin paint brushes across the "S," transforming it into a dollar sign. I placed a few silver dollars · 77

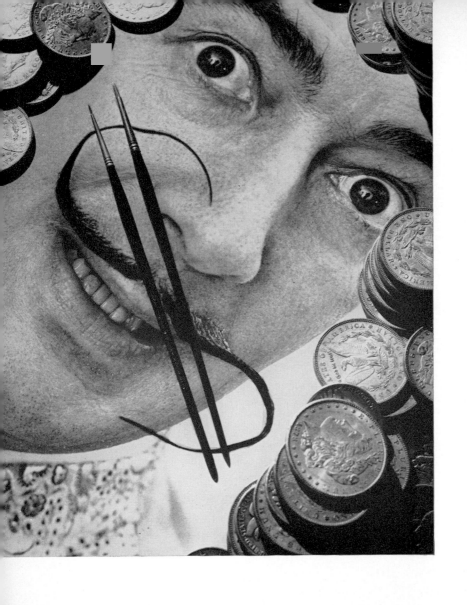

around the print and rephotographed it. Of course, we used it in our book.

The photograph is preceded by the question: "Dali, why do you paint?" The caption under the photograph says, "Because I love art," but the picture shouts, "Money, money!"

Dali, who himself suggested the captions, was delighted. "I have the expression of a little rat. It is perfect."

6. self-stimulation

Scientists have come to believe that our mind works like a computer. In a computer, the electrical impulse travels from one element to another until it produces an answer. Our brain works similarly. The path of the impulse is directed by associations. The more logical our thinking, the more the patterns of our associations become established tracks. The solutions become more and more predictable, which means less unusual and more pedestrian.

This is why a child's brain, where these association tracks are not yet established, often produces such startling and unexpected ideas. Consequently, if we don't want to get a commonplace solution, we too must try to force our thought impulses to travel on new, not-yet-established association paths. We have to scramble up our tracks.

Therefore, my advice is: if you have a problem, don't think about it only during your regular working hours, in the belief that then you are most lucid. Remember or repeat your problem when your mind is partly occupied with something else, for instance with driving a car, or eating, or shaving. Archimedes, who spent many days vainly pondering how to determine the proportion of gold in a crown's alloy, got the solution while taking a bath, and ran out naked into the street, shouting, "Eureka."

You should try to recall the problem while you are tired, drowsy, or before falling asleep. When Newton dozed off under an apple tree, he had been searching a long time for the reason why falling objects did not fly in all directions. The answer came in a moment of drowsiness, when he was hit by the now-famous apple.

During these periods, the problem is pushed into our subconscious where it germinates and ripens. Then, suddenly, a flimsy incident or a passing association triggers the birth of a solution which appears complete like Pallas Athena from the brow of her Father Zeus. This principle of recalling the unresolved problem periodically at different levels of concentration (driving, shaving) or consciousness (tiredness, sleepiness) is what I call stimulation through your own subconscious or, in short, self-stimulation.

I remember that, when for days I tried to invent questions for my Fernandel interview, I could not find one which would precede Fernandel's expression of utter surprise. I knew it had to be a confusing, complicated question, but what should it be about?

One night, I could not fall asleep, ruminating the possibility of a question about psychoanalysis—without any result. Then I thought about modern art, but could not formulate anything that was confusing enough. Exhausted and depressed, I fell asleep.

At four o'clock in the morning the terror-stricken voice of my wife exclaimed, "Who is it?"

"It is I," I answered, grammatically correct. "I just found my question and I am writing it down."

The amazing thing was that I had awakened with the text of the question on my lips. "Don't you think that the superiority of modern art is based on the fact that, by retreating into the realm of irreality, it invades the libido sphere of the subconscious mind?" My mind had continued to work during my sleep. It had combined the two possibilities I had been thinking about and surprised me with the finished solution.

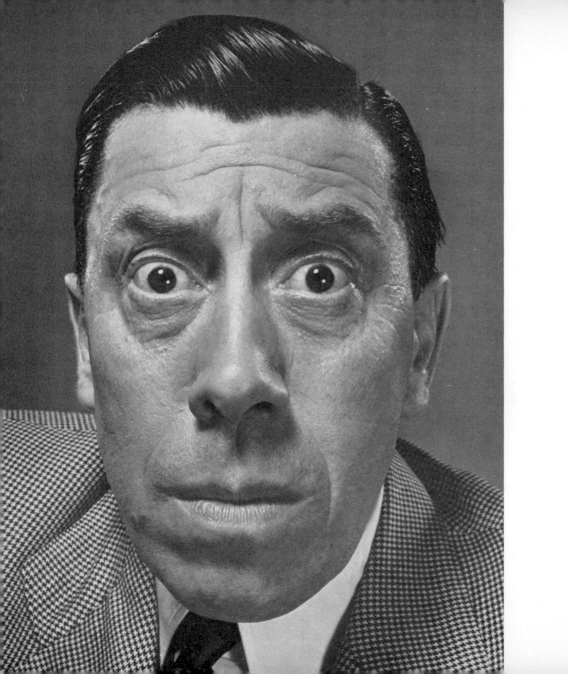

Another time, I was groping for the solution of the following problem. I had always believed that the most important part of a photographer's equipment was his mind. But how to express it in a photograph which I wanted to be a self-portrait? One morning I was brooding over this problem while shaving in the bathroom. Although the bathroom is considered one of the most dangerous places—because most accidents occur there—it is (as most inventors, beginning with Archimedes, will confirm), also one of the most fertile places for the production of original ideas.

Looking in the mirror, I lifted my chin, set the razor to my neck and, suddenly in a flash, had the answer: I would put my head on a tripod, indicating that the photographer's head and not the camera is the principal instrument of his profession.

The six rules and the six kinds of stimulations which I have discussed should not be considered as a purely theoretical treatise on the birth of photographic ideas. **conclusion** Their obstetrical potential can be put into practice. It has helped a number of other photographers groping for new ideas but suffering from a temporary sterility of the mind—alas! a very common disease—and it can help you.

If in the near or distant future you find yourself struggling with a problem but incapable of producing a satisfactory solution, try this:

1. go to your book-case
2. open this book from either the front or the back and
3. cast a glance at either the Table of Contents or at the Index of Rules and Stimulations.

index

rules

stimulations

Philippe Halsman

Philippe Halsman's photographs have appeared on the cover of *Life* magazine no less than eighty-seven times. His assignments for that magazine and for thousands of other clients have made him one of America's most sought-after photographers.

A native of Riga, Latvia, Philippe Halsman began his cosmopolitan career by studying engineering in Germany. He soon turned to photography, however, and settled in Paris. Over a period of eleven years he was one of France's most expert photographers. At the beginning of the Second World War, he came to the United States.

In 1945, Philippe Halsman was president of the American Society of Magazine Photographers. He held that post for a second term in 1954. Magazine work, advertising, fashion, and reportage have been his special fields. His portraits, of course, have won international fame.

Halsman on the Creation of Photographic Ideas will be his fifth book. He already has to his credit *The Frenchman, Dali's Mustache,* a children's fairy tale called *Piccoli,* and the recently published *Jump Book.*   **91**